Dolls and Puppets

Queen Mary's dolls' house

Mary Cockett

Dolls and Puppets

DAVID & CHARLES
Newton Abbot London North Pomfret(VT) Vancouver

To Roma, with love

0 7153 6311 5

0715363115

© Mary Cockett 1974

*Set in 12/14pt Garamond
by Avontype (Bristol) Limited
and printed in Great Britain
by Biddles Limited Guildford
for David & Charles (Holdings) Limited
South Devon House Newton Abbot Devon*

*Published in the United States of America
by David & Charles Inc North Pomfret
Vermont 05053 USA*

**Published in Canada by Douglas David &
Charles Limited 3645 McKechnie Drive
West Vancouver BC**

Contents

Dolls

Puppets

1
To look at,
to play with

Dress is your ruling passion.

The one you trust
Will prove unjust.

By thy lucky star I see
Wealth, love and happiness for thee.

You could hardly be expected to guess where these quotations were found. They are not out of a *What the Stars Say* column in an old magazine or newspaper. They come from a much odder place. Peering through a glass case, you can just read them on a doll's skirt. It is the many-pleated skirt of a fortune-telling doll in the Castle Museum at York.

This is a curio, a surprise, but there is more to dolls than you might think. This book is concerned with what

The many-pleated skirt of a
fortune-telling doll

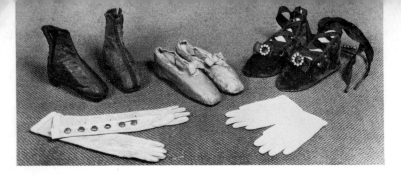

Collection of shoes and gloves from the late nineteenth century

dolls mean, what they have been used for, and what they are made of. There are many books already about how to make dolls, and some about collecting them.

Antique dolls are too expensive for most of us to collect now, but there are adults who, interested in their history or their costume, go on collecting all their lives. And not dolls only, but miniature jewellery and accessories such as gloves or shoes, or dolls'–house furniture and fittings. Some beautiful seventeenth- and eighteenth-century tiny furniture, sometimes in silver, was never intended for play or for children. It was made as a sample of full-size furniture that could then be ordered. The little model was easy to carry about, and its very smallness perhaps made it more wondered at and loved, as people love kittens, puppies, foals, lambs, babies. And dolls? Is this partly why we like them?

Little children want dolls they can play with, dolls to love, and in big twentieth-century toy shops there is a wide choice. Most people are better paid than they were fifty years ago, children have more toys, and a doll, even if it is expensive, is a present that is usually bought, not made. To a small child a home-made doll, given at the right time by the right person, can mean as much as any manufactured doll. An older child is likely to prefer a bought doll for a present, partly because that is what her friends have, but

8

her old dolls, home-made or factory-made, will not go out of favour. Any doll she makes herself will have a special place.

If you had dolls, ask yourself what they meant to you when you were little, and what they mean to you now. If one was more important than the rest, do you remember why? What was it made of? If there was one you disliked, do you know why that was?

Many of the finer antique dolls that have survived to live in museums were owned by wealthy families. Even so, some were probably regarded as 'best' dolls and brought out only on special occasions. They missed the richness of everyday, the rough and tumble of being an ordinary doll, if there is such a thing as an ordinary doll.

Many modern dolls, turned out by the thousand, are cheap looking without being cheap to buy. The child takes

Left. Rag doll from Hamleys toy shop in London
Right. Sasha dolls by a Swiss designer, Sasha Morganthaler

a doll home, and there it will, with luck, have more clothes made, clothes for it alone. But the garments are only a beginning. Gradually it will become a part of the life of the human family. It will have a personality, for its owner, who will probably have quite forgotten that there were other dolls that were almost identical, so nearly the same that it was hard to choose.

There are, of course, *some* expensive modern dolls that will live on, like good art, and take their places in doll history and museums.

Look in a big toy shop or in an illustrated catalogue, and it is soon clear that modern dolls can be divided into two main categories: dolls to look at and dolls to play with. Play dolls can be as big as a two-year-old child—though why, unless for practising babycraft, it is difficult to say—or they can be smaller than a baby's little finger. These tiniest dolls may be family figures to inhabit whatever is used as a dolls' house.

The dolls' house may be anything—just a large cardboard box, or a two-room house with a front that closes, or an open-sided building with several rooms. This last kind is often seen in infant schools where the furniture and dolls are moved by different hands every day. Somewhere now there may be a dolls' house that is gradually being fitted out perfectly and will one day stand in a museum or a large house which the public can visit.

In Yorkshire, at Nostell Priory (which is a house, not a priory), there is an eighteenth-century dolls' house on show. It was designed by the great architect, Robert Adam, and made by the estate carpenter in the 1740s, probably for the children of Sir Rowland and Lady Winn who built the main house.

A world famous dolls' house of the twentieth century is

Interior of dolls' house at Nostell Priory

that designed by a top architect, Sir Edwin Lutyens, furnished by top craftsmen, and presented to Queen Mary in 1924. Visitors in thousands go to see it in Windsor Castle, and whole books have been written about it. It is far from being a play house. Imagine a dolls' house with a water system, where the queen's bath is made of alabaster and fills from silver taps, where the bathroom floor is of mother-of-pearl and there are paintings on the ceiling.

But there are no dolls in this perfect house, only a few miniature guards outside it. According to the *New York Herald* in 1922, there was to have been a royal family of dolls, with their staff. 'Kept in drawers will be two Prime Ministers, a Lord Chancellor, a General. . . .' So it goes on, and the list finished with 'a journalist and a royal aunt'. The dolls in the drawers were to be 'fetched out only on state occasions'.

A very different and personal house is the work of Miss Graham Montgomery of Kinross, Scotland. She went on fitting up her Elizabethan-type dolls' house for fully sixty years, and it holds more than a thousand items. But such creations are exhibition models, not toys.

There were fully equipped dolls' houses and kitchens in the seventeenth and eighteenth centuries. Many were made at Nuremberg in Germany, and they were partly regarded as educational toys. It was thought good training for the little housewife of the future to have a toy kitchen stocked to the last detail with furniture and utensils, but the miniature contents were of such fine quality that they were models rather than toys, and their owners were often adults.

By the nineteenth century the houses and shops were for play, equipped with mass-produced goods, and inhabited by tiny play dolls. The clothes for dolls of this size were often stitched on, not made for regular putting on and taking off. The dolls were characters, with a part to play in their home.

In the present century larger modern European dolls, except for those in national costume, are made for everyday play. Dolls' prams are advertised as 'just like mummy's'. The catalogues show a rich, glossy kind of life. Even the 'pretend' stove, in strong polystyrene, has switches that operate clock and oven lights, and the rings are removable. There is the same realistic approach in the dolls themselves. They are made as lifelike as possible, but this struggling for realism is not new. In 1861 H. Pierotti of Oxford Street, London, whose family had been making dolls for generations, had a printed handbill which advertised his large new stock of toys, including:

Such beautiful Dolls that will open their Eyes,
You may wash, comb and dress them, and not fear their cries.

Many play dolls now can be undressed, fed, bathed, shampooed, even potted, and put to bed. This serious playing goes on every day, as the little owner gives the doll a life, often the same sort of life as her own. Many children find great pleasure in being parents to their dolls—loving sometimes, cross sometimes. On other occasions the same doll is not the child's 'baby', but a friend to talk to, someone who brings comfort by her presence.

Baby dolls are made especially soft and cuddly. Some modellers have searched among works of art for their ideal baby. Käthe Kruse, a German sculptor's daughter, found hers in the *bambini* (the babies) of the Italian della Robbia sculptures. One of the best-known dolls in the world is the Bye-Lo Baby or Million Dollar Baby. Grace Storey Putnam designed the original after searching through maternity hospitals for her model. When she found what she thought was a perfect-looking three-day-old baby, she copied it in wax. That was only the beginning. Then the

Bye-lo baby, designed by Grace Storey Putnam

manufacturers began to think how they could make a doll that would cry just as a baby of that age does, how to give it eyes that would open and close and look like the eyes of a real, very young baby. It took a long time.

Some dolls, aided by a battery, laugh if they are bounced on the knee, walk across the floor, 'speak' certain sentences. They are made as real as they can be, but some children feel they are false and cannot love 'dolls with works in them'. They prefer to accept the doll as a doll, and add to it from their imagination. The speaking doll is not a new invention. More than a thousand years ago there were dolls that could

Rare Parian doll in fine porcelain.
Eighteenth-century French costume

squeak or 'speak' when they
were squeezed: they had bellows instead of batteries.

Some modern dolls have
neat, slim figures, easy to
design and make clothes for.
It would take a good dressmaker to clothe a doll as ele-
gantly as this French boy doll,
who is wearing the garments
that were made for him in the
eighteenth century. He clearly
was never the sort of doll a
child could play with, tuck up
in bed, take on holiday.

Notice how few boys dolls there are. They exist in dolls'
house families, of course, but they are rare in larger sizes.
Boys were not, until recently, and except for teddies and
golliwogs, encouraged to play with dolls. Teddies really
were a new invention seventy-odd years ago. Many mothers,
perhaps most mothers who used to think it girlish for little
boys to play with dolls, were happy to give their sons
teddies. Many adults nowadays still keep their teddies.
There is no secret about Sir John Betjeman's 'Archibald,
my safe old bear'.

Should we ever have had teddies, one wonders, if
American President Theodore Roosevelt had not gone on a
particular hunting trip in November 1902? There, a baby
bear came within easy shooting distance, but the President
did not fire. Clifford Verryman drew a cartoon picture which

appeared in the *Washington Post* and was noticed by Morris Michtom who was not then a toy maker. He saw possibilities ahead, made a cuddly bear, and asked permission to use the President's pet name, Teddy. Here was the beginning of a big business, the Ideal Toy Corporation of New York. Teddy has been with us ever since, in many sizes and even many colours.

A modern doll figure for boys is Action Man, a plastic doll with fully movable joints. He first appeared dressed as a soldier, but later went on to have various costumes—for skin-diving, skiing, and other sports.

Whether you are looking at him or at an ancient doll, try to see what they reveal about the times in which they were made. What was the designer aiming at? Did he achieve it? Was there more interest in the making of the doll or the clothes? Are the clothes well designed, and are they well stitched? Is there any garment there that you could not have made yourself? There was nothing very special in the manufacture of the little Dutch dolls that belonged to Victoria, before she was queen. But look at the sewing done by her and her governess for the more than a hundred dolls that are on exhibition in the London Museum. Look, but you may not envy her the length of time and the effort she must have used in doing her needle-work.

This trio of English painted wooden dolls (from the

Victoria and Albert Museum, London) belong to about 1740—a lady, her little girl, and a nurse. The child doll, in face and in clothing, looks like a little adult. It was not common until almost the twentieth century for dolls' faces to be made to look young and childlike. Children were not merely dressed in adult fashion. They were expected to behave like adults too. Most were not free to play in the way that most of you are. They worked from a very early age in mines, factories, workshops. A newspaper report of 1907 refers to children of perhaps only eight or nine regularly hawking toys, including dolls, in the streets of London. Some of the little dolls they sold were then four-a-penny. They must have had to sell large numbers, before they earned a penny for themselves.

Perhaps large numbers of dolls were bought. Certainly the output from some factories seems very high. One London factory in 1871 was producing 20,000 wax dolls a week.

Besides the doll we started with, the fortune teller, there are other novelty dolls which were made by adults, perhaps for adults. They would not serve for children the same purpose as the cuddly doll, which receives love, and makes a child feel safe or less lonely. Some of them are only gimmicks, some clever bits of mechanical invention. Here are a few, and museums will have more to offer:

pincushion dolls—china doll to the waist and padded skirt below;
dancing dolls—wind the key, and the doll, who may have a partner, dances on a little platform, often to music;
dolls that can sing patriotic songs;
doll dressed in Japanese costume, and 'pouring' tea, then handing it to the visitor;

16

a charity doll who takes your penny in outstretched hand and raises his hat to thank you;

dolls playing musical instuments, pushing a cart, riding a bicycle.

After these curios perhaps it would not surprise you to hear that there have been dolls with two faces. In 1881 Fritz Bertenstein made a bonneted doll which could be smiling or miserable. A pull of a string at the waist produced a crying sound and the happy face disappeared within the bonnet. Luton Museum has a three-faced doll, also German. She shows a sleepy face, a crying face, or a smiling one. Under her bonnet is a knob which controls how she looks out upon the world. There are puppets with two faces too, but there the invention is more suitable, for puppets are actors or ready to be actors.

Different from the automata is the pedlar doll, who will give special pleasure to those who like very tiny objects. She—it is generally an old woman—is dressed in humble costume, and the costume, if it is genuine and given a date, is interesting. Most old dolls wear rather fine clothes. The pedlar doll's head may be made of wood, wax, composition, or—strangely—of a dried apple. But it is her tray that visitors pore over: it may include a net purse, dominoes, a toasting fork, a minute cardboard doll, needles and pins and a thimble, beads, ribbons, laces and buttons, a stamp-size sheet of music, a book, a vase, combs, a watch, or bobbins for lacemaking. This list is only a beginning. There may be more than two hundred objects in her tray or basket.

The pedlar doll is so far from being a toy that she may have been kept under a glass case all her life. If she is dated, we are lucky—well, we are if nothing has been added.

Lace-maker of Bruges.
Late nineteenth century

If she is marked 1830, there should not be anything in or around her tray that was not in use at that date. A magnifying glass is needed to see the detail on some of the objects. You will see among them familiar things, but you will also see objects that were common then and are now almost out of use. You will not have used lace bobbins, but have you ever used a toasting fork—before a coal fire? Somebody called a pedlar doll a social document, and so she is, if the tray has not been meddled with.

As more people travel more children and adults will collect dolls in national costumes. Some are expensive and beautifully dressed, and some, while still expensive, are crude and their clothes are badly sewn. Some costume dolls were and still are modelled on or dressed to look like royalty or other individuals much in the news: they may be television personalities or characters in books. Some such dolls are good in their way, but many are in poor taste. Some of the worst models appear in tourist shops and on stalls near tourist sights. A few streets away, in a real toy or doll shop, you may get better value.

Russian 'nesting' dolls, made also in Poland, deserve a paragraph to themselves. They remain steadfastly much the same as they were in your grandmother's childhood, even though now there are sometimes fewer dolls in the set. Brightly patterned, and quite unrealistic, they are enjoyed by people of all ages. When they cease to be toys to be fitted within one another, they are still gay ornaments. They seem to fulfil both kinds of need, something to play with and something to look at.

Left. Russian 'nesting' dolls

Below. A set of jointed wooden dolls

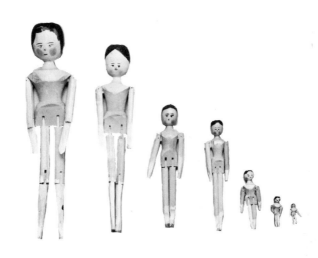

2
What else,
what more ?

It is not known when a doll first became a toy. It is sometimes hard to say now when a doll is a toy and when it is a sacred figure. In Upper Volta in West Africa for instance, children's dolls are sometimes images of Bay, who is regarded as god of the sky and creator of the world. Or the image may be the earth-mother, Kaa-tia.

It seems that early dolls were very simplified copies of the human shape. The doll would not have long, well-shaped limbs, and facial features. It was probably roughly carved in one piece from wood, or it may have been modelled from clay. If you made a doll out of clay or plasticine when you were very young, perhaps you, like some primitive doll-makers, poked little holes for eyes, nose and mouth. The doll probably had, instead of legs, a little dumpy base to stand on.

If you rolled out plasticine and marked out the doll with a sharp instrument, perhaps you gave it arms and legs (simple shapes, like the gingerbread man's in a biscuit

Egyptian dolls, about 1100 BC.
Wooden, with clay faces

Ushabti box containing Ushabti doll.
Ancient Egyptian

cutter). Some children mark out clothes and pattern them, even as these flat Egyptian dolls were decorated. In the British Museum now, they date back to 2000 BC. They are made of wood, except for their faces which are clay.

The Ancient Egyptians and others used to place in tombs objects that were intended to help the dead person in the after life. There were not only swords, jewels, cooking utensils and various household possessions, but also little images specially made to represent servants of the person. They were called Ushabti, meaning Answerers, because they answered every call and did as they were ordered. The Ushabti were not played with: they were not dolls.

Before images were used, huge numbers of people died— were sacrificed with their lords. In accounts of the excavation of the Kings of Ur of the Chaldees of about 3500 BC the evidence is clear. In Ancient China too so many hundreds of lives were wasted in sacrifice at the death of their emperors that the loss to the country was serious. It was Confucius, a wise man and social reformer who lived about 550–479 BC, who gave the order that funeral images (doll figures) should take the place of human sacrifice.

Some figures in ancient graves where children are buried might have been put there because they were loved objects: dolls perhaps, they lie among other toys. Even now sometimes if a child dies a favourite toy is placed with the body.

Nigerian wooden doll   *African fetish doll*

In a part of Dahomey in West Africa, a woman whose child has died buys a doll and wears it tucked in her waistband, as a sign to the dead child that he is not forgotten.

In Ancient Greece and Rome a girl's dolls were buried with her if she died before marriage. On marriage, which then took place at thirteen or fourteen, a girl was supposed to yield up her dolls to some goddess.

In many parts of the world doll figures have been used as magical spirits to ward off evil or to bring good fortune. In some countries a bride was given a doll by her mother until such time as she had a baby. In a part of South America a doll called a *dikori* is carried like a lucky charm, by wives who have remained childless for a long time.

It is not only women who have used dolls as luck symbols. Such an idea is behind some figureheads on ships, and the reason for eyes painted on canoes, eyes which look out for danger and keep it away. Even in this century Eskimos have fixed to their kayaks small doll figures which they carved from bone.

This practice is not dead. Many a person still carries or wears round his neck a little image in human form. It is sometimes just a fashion rather than a sign that the owner has a religious belief. All the same, to judge by the sale of St Christopher images—he is called the patron saint of travellers—many people must have some sort of trust in the power of these tiny doll-size figures.

Doll figures have been used with evil intentions in many countries. Witchcraft was for centuries believed in by learned as well as by ignorant people. In Britain less than two hundred years ago there were examples of doll figures being treated as though they had a life and a power of their own. Known as dolls, poppets or babies, they were made of clay, wax, or even rag.

After various ceremonies, actually called baptism some-times, they were used to try to bring injury or death to a hated person, king or commoner. The doll image was given the name of the person, spells were then said and thorns or pins stuck into the doll where it was hoped that harm would be done to the human victim—in its eyes if the enemy wished him blinded. The persecuted wax image might be held in a fire to melt, in this way draining away the life of the object of hate. Sometimes if he knew of the curse and believed and feared enough, he died. There were, as you might guess, counter spells that could prevent the evil if they were employed in time.

In Japan, as in many countries, dolls seem to have had a religious origin. In the fourth century clay images were buried with the dead. In the sixth and long afterwards dolls were used as scapegoats. Ancient Jewish high priests used to lay the sins of the people on the goat and send him forth into the wilderness. He was called a scapegoat because the sins got away from the people by means of the goat. In Japan, as in many countries, dolls were used for hundreds of years to take into themselves the illness or misfortunes of their owners.

These dolls were not expensive—they were not meant to last. They might be made of straw or paper or slightly carved willow sticks with the shavings used as hair, and they wore paper clothes. Then, ready to serve their owners, and while prayers were said, they were floated out on moving water, and the water helped to wash away the sins or sorrows.

Even dolls themselves have been subjects of religious ceremonies. One school in Tokyo used to hold a Buddhist service for dolls which were beyond mending. They must have been very badly damaged, for Japanese doll repairers are said to be highly skilled.

The little dumpy doll, the *daruma*, weighted in the base so that he rises up again when pushed over, is more than a fun doll. He is a symbol of one who gets up again when life knocks him down, and is presented as an encouraging example to help someone who is ill or has had other bad luck. He is given too as a charm for good health. Mostly now he is a toy, but in Japan and elsewhere in the East, he (or it could be 'she') was regarded as a figure of courage. He was allowed as a toy in China long ago when dolls with limbs were thought—because of their human likeness —to be too powerfully magical for children.

The only example I can find of a human striking a bargain with a doll is in Japanese doll history. The doll was made near a temple in the old days, and then taken home and given a place on the honoured 'god-shelf', whereupon the doll had to 'work' for its owner. The little paper face had no eyes but if it granted the owner's prayers, black dot eyes were painted in. No answer to a prayer, no eyes.

For more than a thousand years the Japanese have held an annual Doll Festival, *Hina Sekku* for girls on 3 March, the third day of the third month. The Doll Festival was, perhaps still is in some households, an occasion when parents prayed for the protection and happiness of their daughters. Families bring out and add to their beautiful festival dolls and miniature festival furniture. Ordinary dolls are played with all the year round, but not these. Some families have treasured these dolls for centuries. Among the most costly and gorgeous are the emperor and empress dolls. The emperor—the real emperor—was long believed to be divine.

Customs vary from house to house, but there is often a little platform draped in red for the arrangement of the dolls. Grand staircases, indoors or out, add dignity and grace to fine houses in many countries, and a model grand staircase is often used for the festival dolls. The attendants, if it is still a court scene, are grouped at the foot of the staircase. The main figures have their place at the head of it, on a gallery or in a palace room, and they stay on display for a week.

On the festival day itself little girls dress in their best kimonos and become hostesses. They offer visitors dainty food on dolls' plates—real, edible food, not the pretty plaster stuff that made Hunca Munca so cross in Beatrix Potter's dolls'-house book, *The Two Bad Mice*.

The Christmas crib is a regular feature in many countries, in churches, schools, and private houses. Sometimes toy dolls and animals are used, sometimes figures specially carved or moulded and used only in that setting once a year. It is a very old custom, as old, some books say, as the celebration of Christmas itself, and that began with Pope Liberius in the year 354. The custom did not spread immediately throughout Italy or to the many other countries that observe it now. Some cribs were and are simple, some very elaborate—crammed with household objects, and the figures wear finely embroidered garments. Travellers to Naples in the time of the German poet, Goethe (1748–1832), and Goethe himself wrote about the splendour of the cribs in the churches.

Another and very different use for dolls was in the world of fashion. Through hundreds of years before the time of dress patterns and fashion books, some dolls were made solely to display clothes for wealthy adults. Dressed in the height of French court fashion, they were sent to England and later to other countries to advertise styles which might then be ordered by rich clients. The garments were perfectly made, and each doll had several sets of clothes.

In the late fourteenth century, Isabella, Queen of England, the French wife of Richard II, received fashion dolls with complete sets of clothes. She was very young, only about twelve, so perhaps the fashion dolls gave her something of the pleasure of a toy too. In that century such dolls were made of wood.

In the sixteenth century the French fashion dolls could be ordered in pairs, one in formal, one in informal dress. They were complete in every detail of clothing and in accessories, and hair styles were always important and up to date.

From the seventeenth century French fashion dolls were sent out to Germany and Italy and Spain as well as England. They went not only to courts but to superior dressmaking establishments. A newspaper advertisement by a London dressmaker stated: 'Last Saturday the French doll for the year 1712 arrived at my house in King Street, Covent Garden.'

In the eighteenth century some of these 'couriers of fashion', as these dolls were sometimes called, were life-size models. It was a life-size model that was sent in 1727 by

Lady Lansdowne to Queen Caroline's ladies-in-waiting. When they had examined it, they were to 'dispatch it to Mrs Tempest, the dressmaker'.

England's dress fashions were highly thought of in the eighteenth century, and her fashion dolls were being shipped to America. The *New England Weekly Journal* of 2 July 1733, carried an advertisement for a Mrs Hannah Teatt, a dressmaker of Summer Street, Boston, to say that a mannequin in the latest fashion had been 'brought from London by Captain White. Ladies who choose to see it may come or send for it. It is always ready to serve you. If you come it will cost you two shillings, but if you send for it, seven shillings.'

The eighteenth-century puppeteer, Martin Powell, small, hump-backed, witty, and never short of an idea for getting himself known, had a fashion doll that regularly crossed from Paris to London and back, showing the latest styles. Such dolls were also used by French hairdressers to demonstrate new hair styles.

By the late eighteenth century engraved fashion plates had been developed. They were easier to transport and cheaper to make than the three-dimensional model, and more people could see them. Even early in the century cut-out cardboard figures were offered with six sets of costumes, so the fashion *doll's* day was nearly done—or was it? For what else really are the fashion models in our shop windows? And there are human mannequins too. With the aid of paper patterns and sewing-machines, large or small, children can make clothes for themselves or for their dolls. Fashion belongs to most people now, not only to high society.

3
Made of what ?

Dolls have been made of a great variety of materials. Modern dolls you can examine for yourselves. You can only look at museum dolls, but the label may have something to tell you about the date, the material, perhaps whose doll it was and how it came to be where it is.

The material mentioned on the museum label may refer only to the head and neck, perhaps the lower arms and lower legs. The rest of the body may be made of something different—cloth, kid, wood, straw perhaps. The label may

Above. Wax doll, stuffed linen body, wearing 'full dress for a lady of sixteen', 1758

Far left. English doll with composition head and stuffed body wearing 'fashionable visiting dress', 1792

Left. English wax doll, cloth body, about 1820

28

show a question mark after the date. It is often not possible to be sure. Moulds for dolls heads went on being used for many years, changed only very slightly and continued in use perhaps by somebody else. Hair styles changed much more often, and it is sometimes possible to date a doll by her hair. Dutch dolls generally keep their stiff, traditional, painted hair style, now and again with other hair glued on top. Some of Victoria's dolls in the London Museum were given ringlets, which were highly in fashion for part of her childhood.

Even the word 'doll' is going to make us pause. It was not used for a toy in England until the end of the seventeenth century. Before then, and later too, they were called 'babes' or 'babies' or 'toy babies', and dolls' houses were baby houses. Bartholomew Babies were dolls bought at the great fair that was held in London for hundreds of years from the twelfth century. Its date was 24 August, St Bartholomew's Day.

When Sir Walter Raleigh went to take Virginia for Elizabeth I, in 1585, an account written at the time says the 'puppets and babes' he presented to the children gave them great delight. In the days before photography and other recording instruments expeditions were accompanied by an artist, and John White was Raleigh's artist on this occasion. From his drawing of a child receiving one of these dolls, it seems as if they were about the length of an adult's hand, probably made of wood, simply carved, and standing not on legs but on the wide wooden stump. In the silhouette view the Elizabethan hat and wide collar stand out sharply.

On the great old London Bridge, the famous bridge with houses and shops on it, there was in 1754 at least one toy shop. From a London Street Directory (Kent's Directory)

Left. Paper figure with five changes of costume: front view
Right. Back view

we even know the name of the shopkeeper. It was Coles Child, and his shop was 'under the sign of the Blew Boar'. In an advertisement listing his goods for sale that word 'babies' for 'dolls' appears again. Since it is only a list, it does not say what the 'babies' were made of.

In most places doll-making is now an industry rather than a craft, but there are still some hand-made dolls. Fashions of country crafts live on for some time after industry has stepped in and organized work on a large scale.

It would not be possible to make a complete list of materials from which dolls have been made. The interested child or adult stretches out a hand and creates a doll from almost anything—pipe cleaners, clothes pegs, wire, gold or silver paper. It may take a long time, and the experiment may be only partly successful, but the doll is her own.

Here is a doll that was created from a dried garden poppy by a child of about seven or eight. The head has a natural, ready-made crown. The arms are a piece of the poppy stalk tied at shoulder level with wool. The skirt is stitched

to paper so that the doll can stand even if the remaining stalk does not reach the ground.

The British Museum has a rag doll, found in Egypt, dating from about 300 BC when Egypt was part of the Roman Empire. It is the kind of rag doll any mother might make. There have been dolls of rag (sometimes stiffened rag) throughout the centuries. Some cut-out-and-sew versions, with features and clothes already coloured in (and colour-fast in washing), make the job an easy one.

Some Ancient Egyptian dolls were made of string. One such doll, dating from about 1900 BC, has a head-dress of bright blue beads.

Bone of various kinds and shapes has been turned into dolls. 'Wish bones' from fowls provide two legs, and heads have been made from sealing wax, which has been available in England for more than four hundred years.

Left. Roman rag doll found in a child's tomb in Egypt
Right. Mexican Aztec doll made of clay

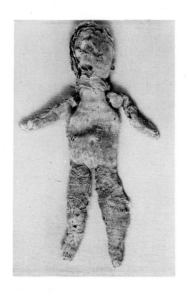 

Clay was used both for grave figures and for dolls. In Mexico the ancient Aztecs made dolls of clay. Six hundred years ago there were German clay dolls with the clothes moulded as part of the doll. Woodcuts of the fifteenth century show a doll-maker at work. Sometimes the limbs were made separately.

Leaf and corn dollies have been made for centuries, and the corn dolly is in fashion again merely as an ornament. In the past she was connected with various superstitions. One belief was that if she was made from the last sheaf of corn in the field, and kept safely throughout the year, the next harvest would be guaranteed a good one. A different sort of corn doll is made from the husk of a corn cob, wrapped with its leaves. These are simple little dolls compared with the intricate folding and plaiting that went into the palm-leaf doll with a fan-like head-dress that was used in Balinese religious ceremony in the nineteenth century.

Wood is still and perhaps always has been used for dolls. Many a child has 'made' a doll by draping a wooden spoon and painting a face on the back of the bowl.

There has been a doll industry in Austria and Germany for hundreds of years. Long before there were doll factories, people living in the mountains carved dolls from fir wood during winter days and sold them in the summer. Nuremberg was a famous early centre for doll-making as it was for the making of soldiers. The term Dutch dolls is known all over the world, but generally they were made in Germany, in Deutschland: the word Deutsch had been slightly changed.

Some sixteenth-century English wooden dolls were turned on a lathe, rather as skittles are, but these were not made by true doll-makers.

The Japanese have done better with their turned dolls, made from hardwood. The head is usually separately made and fixed into a hole in the body, but it can be moved. It is a stump doll: that is, there are no legs—but the 'clothing' goes right to the floor. There are shoulders, but the arms have to be imagined within the painted sleeves. These are ornamental dolls, *unrealistic* dolls. The painting of the head, face and garments is a special attraction.

The Warwick Doll Museum, among its fine collection, has a number of tiny wooden dolls, the smallest less than two centimetres long, and they are not carved in a single piece. Indeed they are jointed at shoulder, elbow, hip and knee, and their faces, lower arms and legs are painted. I have seen in a private house an even smaller jointed doll which rests its elbows on the lower half of a hollowed wooden egg. On the shell of the egg are the words, 'The smallest doll in the world'.

Most larger wooden dolls had painted eyes, but some were enamelled, and even in the seventeenth century there were eyes of blown glass. They have no pupils; perhaps that is why they seem to stare. In England brown was the usual colour, until the blue-eyed Victoria became queen, when blue was the fashion for some time.

Wax was used for dolls in Ancient Greece. It is a material that was used for expensive dolls—in the seventeenth century in Germany and England, for fashion dolls in France. Sometimes the wax was solid and the features were modelled. It was skilled work, but waxworkers had been making figures for church use for centuries. Sometimes the wax was poured into a mould, or used over papier mâché or wood. Often only the head and shoulders were of wax, later the hands, arms and legs. The body was made of stuffed cloth or kid.

Left. Twin wax dolls with stuffed cloth bodies. English, about 1850
Right. German doll. Poured wax head, cloth body, human hair. About 1880

Many wax dolls had their hair inserted in a cut along the central parting, but the split often spread down the face and spoilt it. Eyebrows and eyelashes were sometimes painted on, sometimes inserted hair by hair with a hot needle. The famous Montanari dolls, after 1849, had very natural-looking hair. Augusta Montanari had discovered how to insert each hair separately. Hers is a name to look out for among museum dolls. Have they lived to be on display because they were too expensive to play with? Augusta Montanari won Prize Medal no 122 at the Great Exhibition of 1851, which was held at a Crystal Palace that was built in London's Hyde Park. The judges' report praises the 'lifelike truthfulness' of her 'series of dolls, representing all ages, from infancy to womanhood, arranged in several family groups, with suitable and elegant model furniture'. They praise too the 'variety of expression' for the different ages the dolls are meant to represent.

At the same exhibition the great doll-maker, P. Jumeau of Paris, won a prize, not for the dolls, which the judges thought rather poor, but for the clothes. The report has the moral tone of the nineteenth century, when even stories were meant to teach. 'They might serve as excellent patterns for children to imitate and thus to acquire the use of the needle.'

Often in books about dolls one meets that vague word 'composition'. Perhaps there is no satisfactory word for a mixture. Sometimes only the makers would know the ingredients. Papier mâché (soaked paper mixed with gum or size) was used in several countries for doll making in the eighteenth and nineteenth centuries. The first patent that was taken out in America for a doll was in 1858, for a papier mâché head, the work of Ludwig Greiner, an ex-German. Many excellent puppet heads have been made of papier mâché, and so were the first true baby dolls, at prices ordinary people could pay. They came from Germany in 1850, and were very popular.

There were porcelain heads in the eighteenth century, when the hair was modelled as part of the head at first. Many experiments were made with eyes. Eyes which opened and shut by the balancing of lead weights were a great improvement on those which were controlled by a wire at the doll's waist.

Left. Montanari wax doll, about 1853
Right. 'Ethel', a doll of wax over papier mâché

By the middle of the nineteenth century, first in Germany, a china head was left without the shiny surface. This non-shiny finish is called bisque, and it is almost like a smooth biscuit to the touch. It was usually put in the kiln twice, the second time after the colour was added. Some of the most superior dolls in the world have bisque heads.

By the 1860s the outstanding makers of bisque heads, with necks that could swivel, were French. The Bru family followed one invention with another. Dolls were big

Above Left. Doll with bisque head and arms, kid body and wooden legs. French, Bru, about 1840

Above right. Dress model of figured satin, smocked and trimmed with lace and ribbon. Bisque head. French, about 1883

Left. Two French bisque dolls, Jumeau, about 1855

36

business, dolls and their accessories. Jumeau not only sent their dolls out clad luxuriously, they supplied a trunk, complete with initials, containing other clothes and everything a lady might need to take with her—furs, gloves, jewellery, a writing case too. There were details in these superior dolls of the last century that you might take for granted—the slightly open mouth showing pearly teeth, for example. That was an invention, and still a rarity in the 1880s.

Small china dolls, sometimes called Bonnet dolls when the bonnets were moulded with the head, were made in France, of stone-coloured, almost grey bisque from about 1860. White, unglazed, china dolls of about a finger's length, were made in England from about 1810. Some had jointed shoulders and hips. Some, made all in one piece, were known as pudding dolls because they were hidden, as silver coins are, in puddings for Christmas or other special occasions. They were even used as a novelty by ladies for stirring their cups of tea or hot chocolate.

'Parian' is a word you will be sure to meet in looking at old dolls. It is used for white, unglazed china, but it is a misleading, unsatisfactory word. It comes from the name of a Greek island, Paros, where white marble is found, but Parian figures have none of the translucence of real marble. They are made from a paste that could be modelled to show great detail and set hard. This Franciscan monk, from the Warwick doll collection, has Parian head, hands, and feet.

Many dolls of the past were easily breakable, but many toy makers were doll menders too and there were more dolls' hospitals than are needed now. Charles Marsh of London had been a maker of superior wax and wax-on-composition dolls. His widow, Mary Ann Marsh, continued to run a dolls' hospital. An account in *Strand Magazine*, vol 10, 1895, shows this advertisement.

DOLLY'S HOSPITAL,
FULHAM ROAD, S.W.

Operations Daily from 9 a.m. till 8 p.m.

M. MARSH

Cures all Complaints incidental to Dollhood ; Broken Heads or Fractured Limbs made whole, Loss of Hair, Eyes, Nose, Teeth, Fingers, Hands, Toes, or Feet replaced; Wasting away of the Body restored to soundness ; all Accidents are successfully treated by M.M.

Patients leave the Institution looking better than ever.

DECAPITATIONS AND AMPUTATIONS DAILY.

Heads, Arms, Legs, or Bodies to be had separately. New Heads put upon Old Shoulders, or New Shoulders put to Old Heads. Wigs and Heads for the French Jointed Dolls.

Not responsible for Patients left after Three Months from Date of Admission to Hospital.

CHILDREN'S OWN HAIR INSERTED IN THEIR DOLLS.
Dolls Dressed to Order.
DOLLS CLEANED AND REPAIRED.

114, FULHAM ROAD, S.W.

English cardboard figures with several costumes were used in the serious advertising of clothes more than two hundred years ago. They also led to toy cardboard dolls whose several coats, hats and dresses had fold-on tabs. Fashions found their way into the children's book world too, for example, in *The History of Little Fanny*, dated about 1810. A verse was written about each of the seven cardboard dresses that were sold with the cardboard Fanny.

Japan, too, has paper dolls (with elaborate hair styles) which show children how traditional Japanese dress is worn and how make-up is used.

The list of materials from which dolls have been made is almost endless. Dorothy Coleman, in her *Collector's Encyclopedia of Dolls*, uses nearly seven hundred pages 'to identify dolls through descriptive materials, photographs and marks'. Makers' marks, it seems, may appear practically anywhere on the doll from the top of the head to the side of the foot. Figures may represent a date or they may be only the manufacturer's mould number. There it all is, that kind of detail, if you need it.

Meanwhile, for easier enjoyment, look out for references to dolls in stories, histories, diaries, *and* paintings. The doll is likely to be wearing the same kind of clothing as her owner. Dolls in picture books may also reveal something of the lives of their owners. *Dolly's Picture Book* originally written in German by Rudolph Geissler, is on show at Blaise House, Bristol. This copy of the English version was given to a little girl in 1870. Here is one verse, which has a picture opposite.

Some dollies in carriages tumble about
Until from their elbows the
*   sawdust runs out;*
Some dangle their arms
*   or fall head over heels;*
And some let their dresses
*   get caught in the wheels.*

But the doll in the carriage sits demurely, hands folded in

lap, and not a hair out of place, a model to the children who are taking her out, and the nineteenth-century author meant the moral to sink in to the young reader's mind too.

Another nineteenth-century author, Richard Henry Horne, wrote *Memoirs of a London Doll* (1846).* It is written, as you would expect of a diary or a memoir, in the first person, as if the doll wrote it herself. She is a wooden doll, and so capable of enduring the many accidents that befall her. The author arranges these accidents so that by the end of the book the reader will have had many views of London life, high, low, and middling, through the eyes of the doll. One owner for a short time was a Punch and Judy performer, and she did not much care for being 'in a small box, among a number of dirty old wooden dolls dressed in rags and bits of cloth of all colours'. But she was not there long. The puppeteer sold her to an old–clothes man, but she was not left with him either.

Below. The china doll in Farthing Bundles by Mary Cockett drawn by Jane Paton

Right. American Indian dolls made of wood and cloth

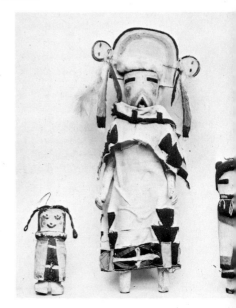

Reprinted 1967, André Deutsch.

Puppets

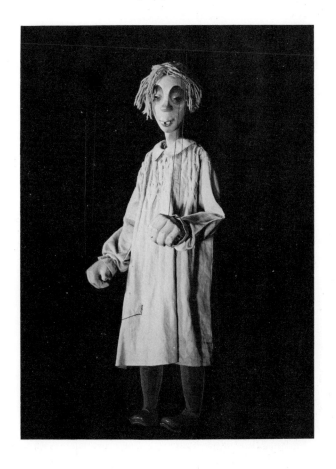

4
Story of puppets

There is a tremendous difference between a doll and a puppet. Between a child and a doll there is often a warm, deep relationship that lasts for years. It concerns only the child and the doll. The puppet is a theatrical creature, and is often surrounded by the many sides of theatre—costume, dance, lights, music, singing, as well as acting.

The story of puppets is a long one. No one knows for certain when they began, and what would be fairly true of one country would not be true of another.

In the British Museum, London, is a Chinese painting on silk called 'The Hundred Children'. It was painted in the Ming Dynasty (1368–1644), and part of it shows children leaning over a theatrical backcloth and performing with

Chinese painting on silk): 'The Hundred Children', dating from the Ming Dynasty (1368–1644 AD). Shows children performing with string puppets while others play the drum and 'clappers'

string puppets, while other children play the drum and 'clappers'.

But there were puppets centuries before this time. They were used in Ancient Greece and Rome. They have been found in tombs—terracotta puppets with articulated limbs and a control rod rising from the tops of their heads. In the fourth century before the birth of Christ the Greek philosopher Aristotle referred to puppets. Five hundred years later the Roman novelist Apuleius wrote about puppeteers: 'Those who control the movement and gestures of the little wooden ones have only to pull a string to move this or that limb . . . in fact the entire body seems to be graceful and alive.' So we know what some of them were made of, and that they were string puppets, and it sounds as though they were imaginatively handled.

Even in these early centuries there were what are called 'stock' characters, basic characters in drama. There was a hunchback with a witty tongue. There was the clever slave who speaks little, knows much, and is ready to say it when the right minute comes.

Sicily is one of the earliest places in which puppetry was performed. The old plays, which are still acted (along with others), are concerned with the struggles between Christianity and Islam, and involve fierce fighting. The

Traditional Sicilian puppet

43

puppets wear armour, lower their visors, draw their swords and advance. Before long, heads and limbs fly and bodies pile up. As the weapons clash, the operators stamp their feet and the barrel organ plays. In Sicily and elsewhere puppets are still used in some religious festivals. In some countries the old plays have been given up in favour of the new. It is important that puppetry, like any art, should be developed, allowing the *best* of the old to remain alongside the new. The new should be looked at carefully too to see that it is not *just* politics dressed up in puppetry.

Puppet figures have had their uses in religion in the distant past. At Heliopolis, if the head priest wanted 'magic' to strengthen what he was saying, the golden statue of Apollo could be made to nod its head.

In Japan puppets of a popular, almost peasant kind (called *kugutsu*), date back to the tenth century. For some centuries these little figures seem to have been used too, almost as charms—to ensure a good harvest, or to keep misfortunes away. In the same way bells were sometimes

Left. Japanese Bunraku Puppet Theatre: Mnjuro, a leading puppeteer, with a female character

Right. Japanese puppet

used, as if they had some mystical power within themselves. These kugutsu, which were operated by wandering players, are not the puppets the country is particularly proud of. Japan has various kinds of puppets, but those most highly thought of are the Bunraku. Some of the plays written specially for these puppets were performed also in the live theatre. A main character needs three operators. They dress in black and stand in full view of the audience, while another person speaks the words, and live music is played. The standard of performance is very high, and the puppets wear splendid costumes.

In India it used to be believed that puppets were holy, that they were little divine creatures. There was also the belief that it was wrong, and dangerous to life, to act, to pretend to be another person. It was considered safe to use puppets because they were not people.

Bill Baird, in *The Art of the Puppet* points out that 'sutradahr' is the word for stage manager in the live theatre in India, and it means 'controller of strings'. As this was the word chosen, it suggests that there were puppets before there were live actors. Note that they were *string* puppets. That there was respect for the puppet itself is suggested by the ceremony that was performed when a puppet could act no longer. Instead of its being given to a child as a toy, as fashion dolls often were in the West, it was floated down a holy river to the chanting of a prayer. In the West sometimes, when a puppeteer has died, his puppets have been buried with him—understandably perhaps, but it was a loss to the history of puppetry.

They could have had a place in a museum. There are particularly famous collections of puppets in the cities of Munich, Moscow, Dresden, Lyons, Chicago and Detroit. In London the British Museum, the Horniman Museum

Wooden puppets from Java

and Bethnal Green Museum have puppets. In a very large museum you may find puppets in the ethnology department, but if time is scarce, ask if the museum has puppets. It may have none, but if enough people ask, it may think of looking out for some. It may, of course, not have been able to buy any. As with model soldiers, many of the best puppets are in private collections. Some museums cannot exhibit everything they have, but if you are really interested, you may be taken into the store rooms.

At the Bodleian Library at Oxford an illuminated manuscript *Roman du bon roi Alexandre* shows two little puppet booths by Jehan de Crise. They look similar to the old type of booth, and the two characters in one of them have a knock-about Punch and Judy look. Notice the castellated

Part of fourteenth-century illuminated manuscript: Roman du Bon Roi Alexandre. *Shows little puppet booth by Jehan de Grise*

edge of the proscenium. Towns were surrounded by walls in those days, and round look-out towers were placed at suitable points on the walls, as they are in the picture. In such booths the puppets were, of course, hand puppets, sometimes called glove puppets.

Before the days when reading and writing were common, bible stories had to be acted, and puppets were sometimes used in church plays. The little dramas actually took place inside the church at first, in spite of the fact that there were some comic characters. A cheeky marionette clown called Grimpesulais acted at St James's, Dieppe, in 1443.

Gradually the plays were moved out of the churchyards, then to the streets or squares. By that time they were not performed by puppets but by men in the various trade guilds. York had about fifty such plays, many of them very short indeed, and not all taking place every year.

Poland, which now has state-supported puppet theatres, showed religious plays by means of puppets more than three hundred years ago. There are descriptions of Italian, French, and English puppet shows in which a net of fine wire was stretched across the front, the whole opening of the stage. Some books say its purpose was mainly to hide the puppet strings, or at least to make them less noticeable. Perhaps, helped by the candlelight and reflectors, the screen added to a feeling of mystery and magic. Perhaps—but this is only a guess—it would be a protection for the puppets if the audience became unruly or too excited, and threw something at the stage.

Puppets have been around and about for hundreds of years, but without being given much chance to develop as they could. The puppeteer has not always known whether he was going to be treated kindly or turned out of town without a chance to prove his worth. The people probably wanted him there, while the church and the magistrates did not.

At Bridport in England in 1630 the puppets were so much enjoyed by day and late into the night 'that the townsmen cannot keep their children and servants in their houses'. At Dover a puppet player was given a shilling *not* to play, to leave the town without giving a single performance.

In sixteenth- and seventeenth-century England hand-puppet shows were given in many towns and villages, and in London in many parts around the city. George Speaight, in *The History of the Puppet Theatre* shows maps of London with the puppet pitches marked. Charles I's statue in Trafalgar Square now stands where an Italian puppeteer, Antonio Devoto, had his pitch.

Shows sometimes took place outside, but often they were indoors in portable wooden sheds. The puppeteer could depend on doing many shows a day at big fairs such as Bartholomew Fair at Smithfield.

In 1684 in London, when the River Thames froze over deeply—as it had done before and as it did later—a Frost Fair was held on the ice. Along with all the fun of the fair, swings and skittle-alleys, horse racing and tobogganing, printing presses to print your name and your handbills on the spot, and men and women selling food from stalls and baskets, there were, of course, puppet shows by day and by torchlight.

Itinerant, that is wandering, players used to try to become, for a while, part of the household of some socially important person, just as minstrels had moved from one lord to the next. It was wise to keep on the right side of the law, which was very hard on anyone who was wandering about looking as though he might be a beggar. A true showman had to carry a licence issued by the Sergeant Trumpeter, but that was not enough. If he wanted to perform in a public place, he had to apply for permission at each town hall, or risk a fine.

Sometimes puppet shows were put on for special occasions such as a mayor's banquet. Town records rarely mention the name of the play. Three favourites, besides *Whittington* were *The Great Earthquake in Jamaica*, *The Blind Beggar of Bethnal Green* and *The Bath Road*. Plays were often based on bible stories, history, legend, or comic opera.

Records give the puppeteer's name and what he was paid. One showman in the late seventeenth century was a Chipperfield, a name that was to be famous in the circus world. Although the puppeteer was often only one among many entertainers—jugglers, tumblers, ballad singers, performing bears and other animals—the show was still known as Punch's show. The crowds were drawn to it by trumpet and drum, and there were other instruments played during the performance.

One famous Punch of the early eighteenth century was Martin Powell, a small, rather hunch-backed man, who had a great sense of show business. He played in fashionable parts of London in the winter and the spring, and then moved on to Oxford, Bath and Bristol. He had more than twenty plays in his repertoire in the three years 1710-13. His puppets were marionettes, and we know that they performed behind a wire 'curtain' or screen. In the magazine *The Tatler* no 44,1709, Richard Steele refers to being able to see 'through the wires that Mr Punch's jaw has a thread which draws it up and lets it fall'.

The Italian Fantoccini puppets were among the best known anywhere, and famous people went to see them—in England, for example, Dr Samuel Johnson, the writer

*Carved and painted wood characters from the Commedia dell' Arte.
Part of a group from the Marionette Theatre in Venice. First half of
eighteenth century*

(who compiled the first English dictionary), the painters
William Hogarth and Sir Joshua Reynolds, the playwright
Oliver Goldsmith, and the composer Haydn.

Those who want to know about Punch in great detail
will need a long chapter or a whole book and there are
several. The first cover of the English magazine *Punch*
(17 July 1841) shows a scene of a Punch and Judy show,
complete with audience, and 'bottler' with drum and pipes
beside the booth. But Punch was a character long before
then. It does not seem to be known for certain where he

'Punch or May Day', a painting by B. R. Daydon, 1842

Punch and Judy

came from. Advertisements of shows—playbills—present him in varying shapes and various costumes with a large stomach, padded hump, nose greeting chin, but sometimes he is dressed as a pathetic, silly character. The Punch that is commonly known in England has all his wits about him, and he wins by fair means or foul. He is a comic who raises laughs among children who enjoy knockabout, but he causes puzzlement and dismay to many children. There is a 1772 English picture of him as he wheels his wife in a wheelbarrow. They fight later, he with a pair of bellows, she with a ladle. The eighteenth-century Punch is less violent than he became in the nineteenth when he batters the baby and throws it out of the window. Judy, who used to be called Joan, has become more of a 'nagger' as time has passed. They are characters who have attracted many artists.

One cannot speak of *the* script of the Punch and Judy play, and many old players probably never even saw a written script.

The Italians had a Pulcinello (various spellings), dressed in white and not pot-bellied in nineteenth-century pictures. They took their puppets to France and all over Europe. The French began a Polichinelle, who had a cat, not a dog Toby. Other countries have figures which are in some way like

Punch or Punch like them—Hanswurst in Germany, Petrushka in Russia, Kasparek in Czechoslovakia, and many another, each with his own individuality and each probably changing with time.

You may have a chance to see foreign puppets here or when you are on holiday in other countries. There is an International Union of the Marionette, known as UNIMA, which has members in more than fifty countries. Perhaps they will visit your country, but language difficulty is a barrier. It must be difficult to decide on performances. It would be a pity if merely dancing puppets were put on because a genuine drama was too complicated, for drama not ballet is the essence of puppetry.

A Japanese Bunraku puppet without clothing

5
Puppet and audience

The relationship between child and doll is mainly a quiet one. The child talks to the doll, of course, as any mother should talk to her baby from the very beginning, but the puppet is not made for quietness.

In thousands of schools today children make puppets. When a child makes or is given his first hand or finger puppet, the relationship may be only between the two of them at first, but it is a relationship of talk and movement. Before long this talking relationship needs an audience. The young puppet–owner—one cannot really call him a puppeteer yet—needs an audience. He or she and the puppet want to act. They want to entertain the audience, to make

Children watching outdoor puppet show

it feel something. They want the audience to respond—to share delight, sorrow, fear, anger, or whatever the drama brings. The child does not say this, of course, but he feels it quite soon.

But puppets are not people, and the good puppeteer knows that and does not try to copy people. Living actors respond to one another. The puppeteer has to work through a constructed object. The real puppeteer, by suggestion and skill seems to give the object a life. He needs physical strength, but even more he needs a vivid imagination. He must transmit through those puppet strings many ranges of feeling, wild fury or the merest sigh.

The face of the living actor can go through many changes —every slight one very noticeable on television—but the face of the puppet is generally fixed. Some jaws can open and shut, some puppet eyes can move, but these are exceptions. There will often be exaggeration, as in a caricature —a big hooked nose will be very big and hooked, a sad look very sad, a fierce eye very fierce. The puppet's whole body, or whatever it has as a body, has to work to impress the audience. The expression 'whatever it has as a body' may need explaining. The puppet may have jointed limbs, or merely head and shoulders and a garment, perhaps with feet stitched on. It may, like some horse puppets, have no legs but instead a full, elaborate skirt that hides the absence of legs. The Kuchi horses, sometimes seen in India, can, in the right hands, buck and jump, sink down, trit trot daintily, or do whatever the situation needs. You may be thinking that, since there are no legs, the audience would sadly miss the sound of hooves, but skilled drummers know how to produce such sounds and how to stir the imagination.

Good work with puppets can leave the imagination stirred

for a long time, so if one puppet show is disappointing or you cannot remember the feeling of it a week after the performance, try another. As in all arts, there is good and bad. A puppet show may be easy to understand and quite pretty, but nothing more unless you are watching to see what the puppet can do. To see how it is worked you would then need to go behind the scenes, but that would be a special favour.

Sometimes, the audience goes to a puppet play it knows well partly because it feels itself a part of the show, and wants the satisfaction of sharing it again along with an audience. Children will ask for the repetition of *Cinderella* or some favourite story time after time, and not children only. Favourite programmes on radio or TV are repeated sometimes because enough people have asked for them. They know what is going to happen, so it is not surprise they are seeking but another 'helping' of the 'cake' they liked before.

Some years ago I arrived in an Italian village where a large marquee stood, and at its opening a board announced a starting time—8.30 in the evening. But of what? On asking the innkeeper, I was told in Italian that the show would not interest me, that it would be crude, rough and ready, or some such expression.

'But what is it? It's not a circus, is it?'

'No, no, but you would not like it.'

'But what are they going to do? Is it a play?'

'Not really. It is a puppet play.'

'I might like it very much.'

'It is not good Italian either. Pooh, you would not like it. It is only for children.'

'Only? Only?' In a country where they love children! 'And starting at 8.30 at night?'

'Well, a few grown-ups perhaps', she admitted grudgingly.

It was a good thing to have persisted. There were a few children, but scores of grown-ups enjoying themselves hugely. They booed the villain, and applauded the brave, whistled at the beautiful heroine, even warned a character who was in danger. The puppets were large, well-handled but heavy marionettes, and the play was obviously a story the adults had known all their lives. They were living through it again with the puppets. But the innkeeper had been apologetic that it was a *puppet* play.

Many people nowadays think that puppets are for the entertainment of children only. It was certainly not always so. In the seventeenth century Samuel Pepys, the famous diarist, went frequently to puppet plays and enjoyed and admired them. On 23 May 1662, after being at the opera 'so silly a play I never saw I think in my life . . . my wife and I to the puppet play in Covent Garden, which I saw the other day, and indeed it was very pleasant. Here, among the fiddlers, I first saw a dulcimere played on with sticks knocking of the strings.' On 21 September 1668, off he went 'To Southwarke Fair, very dirty. And there saw the puppet-show of Whittington, which was pretty to see; and how that idle thing do work upon people that see it and even myself too.' Notice the 'even myself too', for he went to a great many entertainments, and he and the audience were moved, were stirred by the puppet play. 'Idle' had a rather different meaning in those days, not 'lazy', but something like 'small and unimportant'.

Now and again it is an advantage to be small and unimportant. In 1642, during the civil war in England the theatres were closed down, but nobody bothered to stop the puppet shows. The puppeteers were still free to add to their play some little scene that poked fun at those in power. It would have been beneath the dignity of important men to take notice of what a cheeky puppet said. So Punch, or whoever the puppet was, 'got away with' all kinds of personal remarks, and the audience loved it. The puppet was saying, as cartoonists do, something the audience wished they could express themselves.

There are puppets in many countries who comment in this way on current events or make jokes about someone or something. The Javanese puppet character, Semar, had three sons to do it for him—Gaveng, Bagong, and Petruk.

Puppet shows at fairs have been mentioned, but there were times too when they were part of a special evening's entertainment in the houses of the rich. John Evelyn, who travelled widely and kept a diary in the seventeenth century, wrote (1 March 1644 and 20 March 1651) that in France he had seen puppets play in formal gardens and at the start of a ball. He sounds surprised, as though he does not expect to find them there and perhaps does not quite approve. He had seen various sorts of shows already, including puppets and 'mountebanks', outside in front of the Ile de Palais, 'looking on to the great bridge' (3 February 1644), and a performing monkey very fashionably dressed was used here to gather the audience.

On 8 October 1662 Italian puppets which Samuel Pepys had seen and admired, performed before King Charles II at Whitehall. Signor Bologna was presented with a gold chain and a medal worth twenty-five pounds.

The puppeteer performing in the streets could not be sure how his audience would behave. In Henry Mayhew's *London Labour and the London Poor* a nineteenth-century showman talks about his life in a chapter called The Chinese Shades. 'Shades' means shadow puppets, and they were presented in what he calls a Punch and Judy frame.

He thinks, as all comedians must, of what will make his audience laugh, and he gives some examples. A girl, Kitty, is told by her mother not to let the cooking pot boil over, and above all to be sure that the cat does not steal the mutton out of the pot.

Kitty: I'll take particular care that the mutton don't steal the cat out of the pot.
Mother: Kitty, bring up the broom to sweep the room.
Kitty: Yes, mummy, I'll bring up the room to sweep the broom.

'Comic business,' says the showman.

He performed in rich houses sometimes.

We go out two men together, one to play the pipes and speak the parts, and the other to work the figures. I always do the speaking and the music, for that's what is the most particular [important]. When we do a full performance, such as at juvenile parties, it takes about one hour and a quarter. For attending parties we generally gets a pound. . . . If you goes to a gentleman's house, it's according to whether you behave yourself in a superior sort of manner. . . .

There was nothing superior about the behaviour of the audience in certain parts of London.

When we are performing of an evening, the boys and children will annoy us awful. . . . They will have the best places; they give each other raps on the head. . . . I'm obliged to get fighting myself, and give it them with the drumsticks. They'll throw a stone or two, and then you have to run after them, and swear you're going to kill them . . . they spile their own amusement by making a noise and disturbance. Quietness is everything; they haven't the sense to know that. . . . No; girls ain't better behaved than boys; they was much wus. I'd sooner have fifty boys round me than four girls. The impertinence of them is above bearing.

But it was not always children and young people who caused him trouble. On 'Islington-green', while he was collecting money after a performance, some drunken men knocked over the puppet booth while his partner was still inside. It was lighted by candles, of course, and it burst into flame.

In the twentieth century the puppeteer is still hired to give performances at private parties and in halls. He may use Punch and Judy, but he probably has many other puppets. It is to be hoped he has plays as well as dancing puppets.

When your grandmothers were small, many puppeteers earned their money mainly in the summer at the seaside. They put on several shows a day in a pavilion on the pier, or they did even more shows less comfortably on the sands. Every day they put up and took down the booth, the portable stage. As the show was usually Punch and Judy, the audience could follow the story, but often the words were difficult to hear. Sometimes it was the fault of the puppeteer in his use of the 'squeaker' through which he spoke. Sometimes the noise of beach games, ice–cream salesmen and donkey bells got in the way, as well as the sound of the sea itself.

Even well into the twentieth century some travelling showmen used to push their hand-trucks or 'barrows' from village to village in the summer. They might start by train, as Walter Wilkinson did from London on his way to Yorkshire. No taxi to the station for him. He trundled his 'barrow', but first he had to pack it for the summer with tent and sleeping-bag, stove, cooking pots, and clothes as well as with the most important luggage, his puppets.

> *Into the puppet-box went the wooden-headed company, one by one all squashing on top of one another, but all smiling and well stimulated by this absurd idea of running away from London to be wandering vagabonds, not knowing where they would perform next but quite sure that it would be somewhere. They were all in and the lid closed down on them—the new company for the old Punch and Judy theatre—the old country-man and his wife, the hero and the heroine, the cheeky boy, the villain, the fool, the caricature of a parson, a monkey, the two clowns, a ghost, a hobgoblin and Punch himself to act as stage-manager. Poor things! All squashed down in the box with their properties, ready to travel, and like all good actors, willing servants of the public, ready, at a moment's notice, to spring to life and speak their parts.*

Leaving behind him the rich houses where he sometimes performed, he made for the north of England, and wrote a book about his experiences, *Puppets in Yorkshire*, now out of print. He had one or two engagements arranged—to perform in a school for crippled children, for instance, but mostly he wandered, alone. When it was not raining he put on shows on village greens, in market places, fields, or anywhere.

On each occasion he had to erect his booth, and it took time—too long for some children who shouted round his booth, 'banged the curtains, grovelled on the ground to look under them, pitched bits of dirty paper through the proscenium. . . .' He felt angry, but like the good showman he must have been, he turned the situation to his own advantage. When he was ready, he put up a puppet and let it scold the audience thoroughly. After a moment's silence they yelled with delight, and a crowd in front of an auctioneer turned round to watch, so increasing the audience.

It was not until I went round with the hat that they began to turn away, which some of them did marvellously quickly. But not all of them; others took the trouble to come up to me with compliments—and pennies.

Some performers employed a 'bottler', a man to collect while the show was still on, but the bottler had to have a percentage of the takings, and some bottlers were dishonest. One market manager said to Walter Wilkinson, 'If you had a sealed box I might find someone to go round for you. But it would have to be a sealed box.'

All the way through the book Walter Wilkinson is very aware of the audience at his shows. He can feel when he has failed to capture them. The fault may be theirs, but it is he who goes to bed unhappy, and cold, and sometimes hungry. But he starts off again the next day, ready to give pleasure and to feel pleased.

You begin to build up the show under the old Cross, putting your belongings on the worn steps. A boy appears, then a girl. They ask what it is going to be. . . . The children increase, some adults glance at you shyly from the distance, and presently, when all is ready, you retire into your curtains and begin to squeak. The result is marvellous. The children laugh, the adults draw nearer, an upstairs window or two is thrown open, the shopkeepers come to their doors with broad smiles on their faces; more people come into the square, and a party arrives in a car. . . .

After the day's work, 'well and happily done . . . a few children accompany you, and you are glad to have gained their affection'. He used no pet monkey dressed in clothes to advertise his show, no juggler tossing balls in the air, and sometimes with his hand-truck and his old clothes, wet with rain, he was regarded as a tramp or a gypsy.

The one-night stands—performing for one day and then moving on—are very tiring. People who work in puppetry would like permanent little theatres. There is a permanent theatre, The Little Angel at Dagmar Passage, Islington, London, N1. It has a regular company of puppeteers, directed by John Wright, but one-man shows and performances by guest companies are put on too. Puppet shows are given all the year round, twice daily during school holidays and at week-ends.

In Great Britain puppet companies still usually have to take their performances to their audience. The Hogarth Puppets, directed by Jan Bussell and Ann Hogarth, tour in the British Isles and abroad. Two more touring companies are Cap and Bells (Director, Violet Philpott) based in London, and the Caricature Theatre Company (Director, Jane Phillips) based on Cardiff. Your librarian will be able to find the names of the companies nearest to you.

Look out for notices of visiting puppeteers in local papers or at gates of parks and recreation grounds. Every year more councils, trying to keep children off the streets in long school holidays, employ performers to give puppet and other shows. The showman is paid by the council, so

*Pinocchio, a rod puppet from the
Central Puppet Theatre, Prague*

there will be no bottler coming round to you. It is a one-day stand again for the puppeteer, but at least now he is likely to travel with a van rather than a barrow.

In some countries, especially in Eastern Europe, where puppets have been thought important for centuries, puppetry is paid for by the State. Russia has over a hundred puppet theatres. A huge Moscow theatre, altered to suit the great puppet-master, Sergei Obraztsov, has two puppet theatres which seat 300 and 500 people.

Television has brought many changes to puppetry and given it a new life. The screen, like the puppet stage, is small, but it can be deep or seem deep. It is possible for TV to put on plays which the old puppeteer in his little booth would have found impossible—*Peer Gynt* for example, or *Peter and the Wolf* in which characters come far forward through the forest from among distant trees.

The camera can focus on a detail and bring it close before us. Anything that is not wanted can be kept right out of the picture. Lighting is used to produce whatever effect is wanted—dancing sunlight or gloom or mystery, just as the producer requires. Shows for children are generally short, often only a few minutes. Remember the old showman on tour. He went on for an hour or longer sometimes, but he had to be ready to change to suit the audience. He would shorten his programme if the rain came on, or change it if the audience began to look bored, or add something topical or local on the spur of the moment. After several shows a day, and the effort of gathering his own audiences, he must have gone to bed exhausted.

On television we can not only see every detail, we can hear even a whisper, so the performer is able to use different kinds of plays. He has no struggle to make himself heard. His characters do not need to be exaggerated. But unless there is a studio audience, the puppeteer, while being seen by millions of us, will not get the feel of the audience. He cannot hear us muttering at him, but he cannot hear us shouting with laughter either. He will not know if we walk off and make the tea.

But if he misses his audience, at least he can give all his attention to what he is doing. Many people are employed in the making of one tiny programme. If the performance is being filmed, it is even more expensive, but those who are making it will hope to sell in other countries too. Even in its own country the programme reaches at one showing millions of people, not just that little group on the beach or in the market place.

Think how many puppet characters you have known on television since you were small. What is the first you remember? Have you a favourite TV puppet? If you have, why is it a favourite? If you say, 'Zebedee arrived, *ping*,' most of your friends will know who he is. They can probably mention many of the other characters in *The Magic Roundabout*, which is enjoyed by adults and children.

In many countries puppets are used in school television programmes, not only in learning-to-read but in mathematics and wherever in the timetable they have a part to play. Some people think children pay more attention to a puppet than a human being, perhaps because it is little and a novelty and connected with entertainment. What do you think about puppets in educational programmes?

Puppets appear in advertisements too. They are used to catch your attention, but they were used for this purpose long before television was invented. An old watercolour by Grainger, in the British Museum, shows a tooth puller who has employed puppet players to gather an audience. Once the crowd has collected, he hopes to find patients among them.

Did your interest in puppets start with television? Was it continued by your making a puppet at school? If you made a puppet, was that the end? Or did that puppet need an audience? Did you feel that it needed other characters and a scene in which to play? This is where we started this chapter, with the need for an audience.

In a Bristol school I saw by chance a galaxy of puppets in the entrance hall. They included clowns, tramps, pirates, a flower seller, wizards and a witch, Royalty, a fluffy-haired professor with a tiny copy of *Science World* tucked in his white gown, *and* a blue-faced puppet with blue, silver-tipped antennae, a semi-transparent blue nose, and four, not five, spiky fingers. He came from Mars, so he had to be different, I learnt later. The best feature of this rich, first experiment with puppetry was that, though the children had made whatever puppets they chose, they had afterwards created a play and parts of several plays. Drama, which should be at the heart of puppetry, had begun to work.

6
Kinds of puppets

If you hear a person being spoken of as 'merely a puppet', you will feel the scorn behind the words. They will mean someone who is completely under the control of another person all the time, and that is no compliment. If you hear puppets being called little dancing dolls, that is no compliment to puppetry which has its own place in the history of drama.

There are many books about how to make puppets and how to work, operate and manipulate them. There is a skill to be learnt, and often it is not well learnt. It takes a

Children with glove puppets backstage

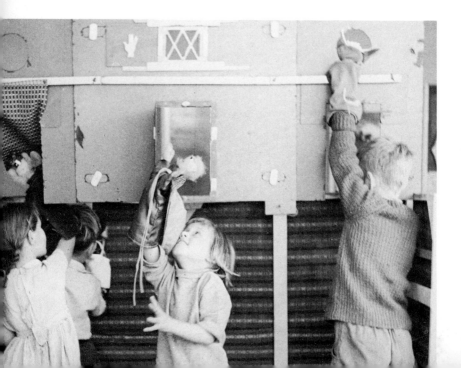

long time too. There are written plays, and plays unwritten which the puppeteers invent for themselves around old or new plots. 'The play's the thing' that matters, once the art and the craft have been mastered.

The hand or glove puppet is likely to be the first kind a young child uses. He is very close to it physically, and he may become fond of it. The first finger controls the head, the thumb and usually the second finger control the arms. It is easy to make such movements as taking hold of something or nodding the head, and this is as far as many children get. Some people make hand puppets with papier mâché heads, shaping the face, creating the character.

Now and again you may see a finger puppet, home-made for a small child's entertainment. A mother may use glove fingers to become the moving legs of a puppet. Or she may make small puppet heads to fit on a finger, and the puppets should move and talk to each other. They probably will if the child has watched a programme as good as the BBC's *Fingerbobs*. Even to the young child puppets should mean drama, though he will not know the word 'drama'. Perhaps you could make such small puppet figures for little children in hospital—for use on tiny fingers, so the loop or finger hole must be very small indeed.

The smallest finger puppet I have seen is in the Warwick Doll Museum. It is scarcely over one centimetre from its chin to the tip of the white pointed cap. It is displayed with a family of pencil-thin rag dolls all dressed in white. Perhaps the child owner was supposed to entertain her solemn-looking family of dolls'–house dolls with this minute puppet.

In shadow puppetry what the audience sees is a shadow of a real puppet that is being worked beyond a screen, a translucent screen like a roller-blind. Behind the puppet is the light that throws the shadow on to the back of the screen:

Javanese shadow puppet

it may be light provided by electricity, or, as often in the East and in the past, by oil lamps or candles.

The puppet may be moved by rods, or by strings attached to a rod. Unless the figures are very simple, they are jointed at the arms and neck and on one leg. In many designs the other leg hides the supporting rod.

Shadow puppets are said to be the oldest kind of puppet, and were in use many centuries ago in China, India, Java, Turkey, and Greece. Children sometimes make them of card or cardboard, but the figures of the East, which were created for long use and for long shows that sometimes lasted through the night, were made of leather. The Field

Chinese shadow puppet

Museum of Natural History, Chicago, has about a thousand shadow figures.

In ancient China ladies were not allowed to attend plays in which the characters were real people. They were allowed to go to shadow shows which they watched from the front of the stage, while the men watched from the back where they could see the performers at work.

The oil lamps which threw the shadow puppets on the screen must have added to the sense of mystery and magic. The rods which controlled Chinese puppets and other puppets of the East were not hidden, as they were when shadow puppetry became a fashion in Europe in the late eighteenth century. That was at a time when silhouette portraits and paper cutting became fashionable.

An eighteenth-century song which became the subject of a shadow puppet play in many countries was *The Broken Bridge*. It is brief and funny, and about a proud traveller who wants to cross the river. Questions go back and forth between him and a workman who is on the other side. The workman tells him the ducks swim over the water, and when the traveller asks how deep it is, the answer comes:

The gravel touches the bottom, tra-la, tra-la, tra-la.

Some nineteenth-century families had shadow shows in their homes. Your grandmother was probably shown how to place her hands together so that they would cast a shadow of a rabbit or a dog's head on a roller blind or a plain wall.

Russia, which takes its puppets seriously, has a permanent shadow theatre in Moscow. The European name that most people known in connection with shadow plays is that of

Shadow puppets in a Victorian home

Lotte Reiniger, who was born in Germany in 1899. Here is a genuine creator. As a child she wrote and illustrated stories. When she told them, she showed pictures too. At school drama was her chief interest. After school she began cutting out silhouette portraits of actors. They were so well done and they showed such sharp observation that they led to work on films at a time when films were new. She made her first of many silhouette films in 1919. When television came, she turned to that medium too and made films for children.

She describes in detail how she works in *Shadow Theatres and Shadow Films*. In constructing an animal figure, for example:

> *You must not only know the skeleton in order to find out*

Lotte Reiniger, shadow puppet 'Carmen'

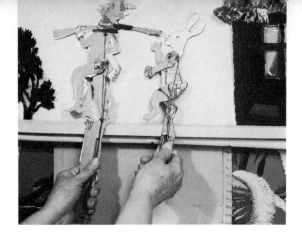

Lotte Reiniger manipulating shadow puppets backstage

the proportion of the limbs. You must also appreciate how the animal moves. You must grasp the rhythm of his motion, register it in your mind and get the feel of it.

She explains that later, when you come to bring life to the creature on the screen, 'you must be that animal, moving as it does. The animation will always be stylised, but this stylisation must be true.' At the zoo, when trying to learn the timing of an animal's movement, she even practised imitating it in front of the cage, to the astonishment of other visitors.

In nineteenth-century England when toy theatres were in fashion, the characters, like many shadow puppets, were

A Pollock's Toy Theatre being manipulated by George Speaight

Rod puppet in the making.
Foundation for the 'Boggle Bird'

cut from card, and they moved along wires. Their price then was 'penny plain' or 'twopence coloured'. Many came from Pollock's, where theatres, puppets and 'Dutch' dolls can be bought today, but the main part of their premises at 1 Scala Street, London, W1 is taken up by a museum of toy theatres. You may find such a theatre in your local museum, given or lent by a local family.

The rod puppet is usually worked from below nowadays, but there are exceptions. The *marotte* is the simplest form of rod puppet, the medieval fool's head wearing cap and bells and fixed on a stick. There are modern French *marottes* which have been given shoulders, arms, and a head that can be turned. Children make simple rod puppets by fixing a stick to the back of a mask.

The rod puppet can be flat or rounded (three dimensional). The rod extends into the head (or the neck can be a spring), and thinner rods can be added to various joints to make them swivel. Head and arm movements can be varied, but the rod puppet does not walk.

Rod puppet completed

If the figure is large, as in some street shows in New York, or if the movement is complicated, more than one person may be needed to move the controls. In such cases the stage may be larger, and the space below stage (for the operator) must be larger.

Detailed information on the history and making of rod puppets is given in Marjorie Batchelder's *Rod Puppets and the Human Theatre*. See too the book by Marjorie Batchelder and Virginia Lee Comer, *Puppets and Plays*, which also has at the end a long list of other useful books on subjects connected with puppetry and suggestions for stories and poems that can be adapted for puppets.

The ventriloquist's doll must be included among rod puppets. Its head movement is controlled by a rod, and its mouth and eyes are movable. The ventriloquist wants you to watch the doll's mouth movements to take away your attention from his own mouth. If you want to try speaking like this form of puppet, there is help for you in Douglas Houlden's book, *Ventriloquism for Beginners*. If you are going to take part in puppet plays, you will need to know how to use your voice. As a puppet actor you are not a normal actor. You have to pretend to be the puppet, to speak in a non-human voice. Showmen throughout the ages have used some kind of instrument—a 'swazzle' in England, a *pivetta* in Italy, in India thin bamboo strips with a 'reed' in between; but these speaking devices are for professional puppeteers.

Perhaps the Jumping Jack should be mentioned, if only because he looks gay and has been in existence for hundreds of years in many countries. One pull at the string on his head, and out go his arms and out go his legs, but his movements are limited and he cannot 'act'. It is hard to know why he has remained in existence for so long. Perhaps

Marionette made by Chris Leith

he lasts long in families because he is not played with.

The marionette is for many people the only kind of puppet that really matters. It is controlled by strings from above. It is harder to make and to operate than other puppets, but it offers greater variety of movement and of feeling. Some operators think they are doing all that is necessary with a marionette when they have learnt how to make the puppet walk, but that is only the beginning. Is it good walking? Does the toe tip down when the knee is lifted? Do the feet stumble over each other intentionally or because the puppeteer cannot stop them? Does he keep one or other foot on the ground, as he should?

The walk must have a meaning in a dramatic sense too. Why is the puppet character walking? How is he feeling? A little tired, or bored, or exhausted to the point of dropping? Has he come far? Is he anxious or angry or in despair? Why is he feeling as he is? He is not a piece of wound-up mechanism. He is an image for the feeling he has to portray, and if his movement looks merely mechanical, the operator has failed.

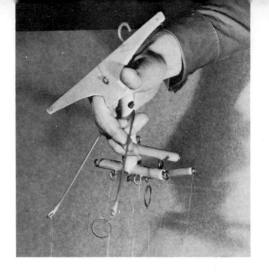

It is work that calls for immense concentration on the character of the puppet and his situation. It needs delicacy and strength in finger, arm and shoulder movements. Make no mistake, it is hard work. The puppeteer is acting through somebody—well, through something outside himself. The puppet will take its life from him, from what he can do with it.

Good puppetry is enjoyed by adults and children. The best puppetry can rouse all the emotions a good live actor can—if the play is right, if the size of the auditorium is right. A full-size theatre is too large. The audience needs to feel close to these generally little characters.

Sometimes the operator does not speak. He performs through his puppet and another person is the narrator. This form of production is said to be simpler than involving the puppeteer in making his words fit exactly with the movement. It may be the only solution if the operator is excellent at manipulating the strings but has no great skill with his voice. But the narrator has to be very good, or some of the drama, the clash between characters, is lost.

The strings are fixed to the control bar, which may be horizontal or vertical. The shoulders, which have to take

the greatest strain are strung first. The neck needs to allow
the head to move downwards or to the side—so, two more
strings. One at the back of the waist allows the puppet to
bow, and there are knee, foot, and hand strings. All have
to be of the right length, neither too taut nor too slack.
Peter Fraser's *Introducing Puppetry* explains clearly and with
diagrams. The number of strings mentioned above may
sound enough or more than enough to manage, but many
Chinese marionettes have twenty to forty strings, some
giving individual finger movements and needing all the
operator's fingers. A juggling elephant has thirty-two
strings. Traditional Burmese marionettes go up to sixty
strings, involving harp-like fingering. In complex stringing,
some threads may be coloured to simplify selection.

Carving wooden puppets

This is just one kind of a great wealth of information that is offered in A. R. Philpott's *Dictionary of Puppetry* which no one concerned with puppetry can afford to be without. It is more than a dictionary, it is an encyclopedia. Unlike many such encyclopedias, it makes very pleasant, lively reading, whether you dip into it, or read it page after page. And it is written by one who has 'lived' puppets for more than fifty years and is internationally known.

A traditional early English marionette

Acknowledgements

The author thanks Mr A. B. T. Hills, Mr R. B. Buckley and the children of Elmlea School, Bristol, who discussed their lively puppets with her.

Grateful thanks are due also to the following bodies and individuals for permission to reproduce the illustrations used in this book:

HM The Queen, frontispiece; Bethnal Green Museum, pp 8, 18, 28, 34, 35 (left), 36; Bodleian Library, Oxford, p 46 (bottom); British Museum, pp 20, 21, 22, 31, 40, 42, 43 (top), 44 (right), 46 (top), 68; Peter Burton, p 11; Jan Bussell, p 77; Castle Museum, p 7; Central Puppet Theatre, Prague, p 63; Hamley's of Regent Street, p 9; Little Angel Marionette Theatre, p 41; Violet Philpott, pp 43, 44 (left), 51, 52, 53, 66, 71, 72, 74, 75, 76; Lotte Reiniger, p 70 (bottom); Tate Gallery, p 50 (bottom); Victoria and Albert Museum, pp 15, 19, 50 (top), 70; Warwick Doll Museum, pp 14, 30, 35 (right), 37
The line drawings are by Janet Duchesne.

Index